Foundations of Freemasonry Series

The Doorway of Freemasonry & The Mason's Apron

Two Essays by
William Harvey

Foundations of Freemasonry Series

The Doorway of Freemasonry & The Mason's Apron

Two Essays by
William Harvey

Lamp of Trismegistus
NEW YORK . GENEVA . BEIJING
WELLINGTON . KANSAS CITY

Copyright © 2013 Lamp of Trismegistus

All rights reserved. No part of this publication may be reproduced or transmitted in any form or by any means, electronic or mechanical, including photocopying, recording, or by any information storage and retrieval system, without permission in writing from Lamp of Trismegistus. Reviewers may quote brief passages.

ISBN: 978-1-63118-001-9

The Doorway of Freemasonry

PREFACE

The following pages seek to do something towards explaining the origin and meaning of the word "Tyler", and also to describe the duties that appertain to the official who guards the doorway.

In olden times, the Tyler was a picturesque character, and the symbolism of his office was not always appreciated. I hope what I have been able to glean from bygone records may be of real interest to members of the Craft.

4 Gowrie Street, Dundee.

THE DOORWAY

The Tyler is the last official who is invested with authority at the ceremony of installation, and the words which are addressed to him by the presiding officer may serve as a text upon which to hang a few remarks on the office, its history and its functions.

Brother Tyler, says the Installing Master, I commit the Sword into your hands to enable you effectually to guard against the approach of cowans and eavesdroppers, by which we are reminded we ought to prevent the approach of every unworthy thought or deed, and to preserve a conscience void of offence towards God and towards man.

Now, the first question that is likely to suggest itself to the student of masonry is, "What is the meaning of the somewhat strange title that is applied to the doorkeeper of a lodge?" And he will find it rather difficult to get a convincing answer. Like many other things in masonry the title appears to be Scottish in its origin, and most authorities at vague in their explanations, If we consul "The Pocket Lexicon of Freemasonry," compiled by Bro. W. Morris who boasts the Eighteenth Degree and describes himself as a "Past Inspector General of the Royal and Select Masters" we shall be told that a Tyler is

> *"an officer of the Lodge whose duty it is to keep off all cowans and intruders from masonry, and to see the candidate for masonry comes properly prepared.."*

It seems a poor achievement for a man who has climbed to the Eighteenth Degree to have acquired a stock of Masonic lore so slender as that indicated by such a definition. Any Entered Apprentice could probably tell us as much. If we turn to Lloyd s "Encyclopedic Dictionary" we find that the main word is "tile," which is defined as "the door in Freemason and other lodges," and the compiler tells us that the etymology of the word is doubtful. The dictionary says that, used as a verb, the word in Freemasonry means "to guard against the entry of the uninitiated by placing a tiler at the door", and that the phrase "to tile a lodge" means, figuratively, to keep secret what is said or done. All this does not carry us very far. The Rev. A. F. A. Woodford, author of "Kenning's Masonic Cyclopaedia," says that the word comes from "tegulator," the Latin term for a workman who lays tiles, and Albert Mackey in his "Lexicon" says:--

> *"As in operative masonry, the tyler, when the edifice is erected, finishes and covers it with the roof, so, in Speculative Masonry, when the Lodge is duly organized, the Tyler closes the door, and covers the sacred*

precincts from all intrusion."

I must confess that I have some difficulty in following the argument that the man who guards a door is connected with the man who covered a roof. To me there seems no natural connection between them and I think we must look elsewhere for the origin of the designation. In olden Scots the word "tile" had a wider meaning than that of merely referring to the roofing of a house. To tile a thing was to cover, or hide, or keep it secret, and in this sense -- without any reference whatever to the covering of a roof -- it quite appropriately applies to the intention of Freemasons to guard their mysteries from the uninitiated. If this be correct, the masons would find that the most direct way to secure secrecy was by keeping the lodge lockfast, and in process of time the man whose special duty it was to attend to the door -- the man who tiled it -- would come to be known as the tiler.

But there are two other possible explanations both of which I submit with all deference, and rather as contributions to the discussion than as final pronouncements. One is that the word may be derived from the calling of the man who filled the position; and the other is that it may have originated from one of the important duties which he discharged.

To begin with, we must bear in mind that the office is the humblest in the Lodge, and was invariably assigned to a poor brother who was recognized as in need of the salary attached to it. Now, in many of the old operative lodges, tilers were associated with masons because theirs was an allied trade; but I presume the tilers would always be few in number, and probably were very poorly paid. My theory is that the masons, none of whom may have been anxious to become the servant of the others, may have bestowed the salaried office upon one of the tilers partly because he followed a different occupation and partly because he needed the remuneration which went with it. If this theory should happen to be the correct one, the origin of the word "tiler" instantly appears.

My other explanation is connected with the proverbial phrase, "It takes nine tailors to make a man." If we translate that into Scots it becomes "nine tilers to make a man," and it is worth while looking into the origin of the saying. It is believed to have nothing to do with the knight of the needle; but to refer to the tolling of a bell in the case of death. Formerly at the death of a man the tolling bell was rung thrice three tolls; while at the death of a woman it was rung only three times two tolls. Hence nine tolls indicated the death of a man. Halliwell gives telled-told, and a tolling-bell is a teller. In regard to "make," it is the French word "faire", as "On le faisait mort, that is some one gave out or made known that he was dead." One of the principal duties of the tyler in earlier days was to warn brethren to attend the funerals of deceased craftsmen. Thus in a very practical sense he gave out or made known that a brother was dead. Like the bell he became a "teller," and it may be that in this way his office got its name. I have not discovered when the word was first used in Freemasonry, but its introduction is comparatively modern, for the Tyler of today is the descendent of the "officer of bye- gone years. In all Scottish burghs there was the town's officer who carried out the instructions of the provost; there was the guildry officer who obeyed the behests of the Dean of the Guildry and his council who represented the merchants of the burgh; and each incorporated Trade, or association of Trades had its officer who attended upon the Convener and his Court. One of the trades of all the burghs was the masons -- I mean the operative masons -- and this trade, like the others, had its officer. When it shed its purely operative character, and assumed the complexion of modern Freemasonry, it retained its officer who has descended to our own time as the familiar tyler.

But long after Speculative Freemasonry came into popularity, the door-keeper continued to be known as the "officer," and this, I think, proves that the designation "tyler" is of comparatively recent use. He was a picture-esque character in the good old days just as, sometimes, his fellow-officers of the town, and guildry, and trades were and continue to be. At Stirling the town s officer is clad in scarlet coat and trousers, white stockings, shoes with silver buttons, and a cocked hat. The beautiful and picturesque raiment is said to be of French origin introduced by Mary of Guise about the middle of the sixteenth century. The burly officer is a gorgeous personage to look upon, and there is a tradition that when some distinguished aristocrats visited the won they bowed most obsequiously to him under the impression that he was the provost of the burgh! The Guildry officer was clad in green coat and trousers with white stockings and black shoes with silver buckles. His attire was completed by a silk hat encircled with a gold lace band. The Trades officer also was garbed in a striking fashion. What is true of Stirling is true of many other burghs, and most likely accounts for the fact that the Tyler of the Mason Lodge was often very grotesquely clad. For instance, we find from the records of "Mary s Chapel" No. 1, that in 1770 that Lodge decided the Tyler

> *"should get a suite of Light Blew Cloathes suitable to the collour of Cloathes suitable to the collour of the Lodge Ribbons, with a silver Lace round the Neck and Cuffs; also a Hatt with Silver Lace, Button, and Loop."*

This raiment continued to adorn the Tyler for over forty years, and must have added a touch of color to Masonic processions of the period. In 1813 the question of renewing the officer s dress came before the Lodge when it was agreed that a blue coat and a cocked hat, richly trimmed with gold lace, should be purchased for the tyler to be worn at the procession on St. Andrew's Day.

But this raiment appears commonplace beside the gorgeous uniform of the Tyler of Lodge Scoon and Perth. In 1745 the brethren of that lodge lamented that their officer, being "a poor man," frequently attended the meetings in torn clothes, and instructed the Treasurer to procure him a new coat. This doubtless made him respectable for the time being, but in the beginning of the nineteenth century -- probably copying the example of Mary s Chapel -- the brethren yearned for something distinctive. And nothing less than the style of a Grand Turk would satisfy them. The Treasurer and a committee were appointed "to get the dress done in a masterly" fashion. It consisted of white trousers -- which were washed from time to time at a cost of sixpence -- a royal blue velvet tunic with a light blue vest on which were embroidered in whiter the name and number of the Lodge. There was also a royal blue cloak trimmed with ermine, and the headgear was a feathered turban. To add to the ferocity of the Tyler s appearance a pair of moustaches were supplied, and at a later date a beard was added. Armed with a curved sword of ample dimensions, the functionary looked a very formidable person to be regarded with fear and awe.

I have no doubt that many other Scottish lodges attired their tylers in distinctive dress. In examining the minute books of Lodge Ancient, Dundee, I found that an inventory taken on 2nd January, 1812, included a suit of Tyler s clothing which consisted of a coat, vest, kilt and bonnet. No particulars are given as to color or style, but on 3rd January 1816, a bonnet was produced for the use of the Tyler. The Committee were highly pleased with it, and agreed to purchase at a cost of thirteen shillings sterling from which one may conclude that it was no ordinary piece of head-gear.

The duties of the officer of tyler in Jedburgh in the middle of the eighteenth century fell to the youngest apprentice, evidently on the same principle which provided that the youngest tailor should "carry the goose." But the youngest apprentice could compound by paying sixpence a year so long as he remained last entrant, and that he generally did so is seen in the fact that the Lodge had a regular officer who drew the amazingly important "sellary" of half-a-crown per annum! Fifty years later in the same lodge, William Cook, an auctioneer by profession, bound himself to act as officer for three years in consideration of the gratis entry of his son. At Dundee the Tyler had more substantial emoluments. The brethren of St. David's Lodge, who were chiefly business and professional men, contributed one shilling each per annum to the officer, and in addition he had a recognized scale of perquisites from every new member. And he got a dram along with the others. The expenditure for 1776 includes "one shilling on eight different occasions for a bottle of punch to the tyler."

At the present time the Tyler, practically speaking, is the only paid official of a lodge. The

Secretary and Treasurer receive honoraria from time to time, and the Master has his labors recognized when he leaves the chair. But all these things are in the goodwill of the brethren. Not so with the Tyler. The nature of his work debars him almost wholly from mixing in the social life of the interior of the lodge and this, together with the fact that, in former times, he was more or less the personal servant of the R.W.M., of the deacon as the R.W.M. used to be called in operative masonry, led to his being paid for his services. Today, as a general rule, the Tyler s remuneration takes the form of a fixed sum -- usually a shilling -- for every initiate. This is not always a fair way of payment for, if, in the course of a year, there are few candidates the Tyler's wages are reduced though his work may not be greatly lessened. But the system has all the authority of age -- is, indeed, one of the ancient landmarks of Masonic finance -- and none but bold men would dare to suggest an alteration.

    I find that, in former times, while the system was the same, the sum paid was considerably larger. The ancient lodge or craft of operative masons in Dundee who received a charter of incorporation from the Town council in 1659 appointed six brethren to frame rules and regulations. These byelaws, which were duly approved by the Lodge, set forth,

> "every entered apprentice shall pay to the officer 6s 8d at his entry and when he is

17

passed 13s 4d, and when he is admitted free master 13s 4d."

These figures, of course, refer to money Scots which was only a twelfth of the value of money sterling.

When we come down to Speculative Freemasonry we find the sums much reduced though here it is money sterling and not money Scots which regulates affairs. St. David's Lodge (No. 78) which was instituted in 1759 charged an initiation fee of £2 5s, of which sum the officer received 1s 6d. when a candidate was initiated and 1s when he was raised. The circumstance that he got nothing when the member was passed is probably explained by the fact that, as a rule, a member was passed and raised on the same evening.

When Thistle Operative (No. 158) came into existence in 1785, it introduced a new feature into Masonry in Dundee, and added to the duties of the Tyler. It set up a benefit section, very similar to the work now discharged by Friendly Societies, and undertook to see deceased brethren properly and decently interred. One of the byelaws provided that the brethren in town and suburbs were to "attend the funeral in clean clothes," under the penalty of sixpence each if they could not give a proper excuse. The officer's duty was to summon them to attend, and for this he was "paid his day's wages off the Lodge."

In one respect the Tyler is the equal of the

master and in another he is, indeed, the Master's superior. Both are equal in respect that each receives a gratis invitation to any social function in connection with the Lodge. The reasons for this are very different. As a rule in Speculative Freemasonry in bygone days, the duties of Tyler were undertaken by some brother who was not too well endowed with worldly goods, while the honor of Master was enjoyed by some lord or earl who looked in upon the lodge only at long intervals. Naturally this figure-head was expected to grace the annual festival, but the request for his attendance would be put forward with becoming humility and his presence regarded as a favor. Consequently no suggestion of payment for admission would be made; and on the other hand the Master would doubtless spend his money very freely during the night. The Tyler was at the other end of the social scale. The comfortable burgesses and county gentlemen who formed the lodges would never dream of asking their humble officer to be out of pocket, and so he got his place at the table without money and without price. The Tyler is the superior of the master in this respect that while no brother can be R.W.M. of more than one lodge at the same time without dispensation from Grand Lodge, the Tyler can be -- and frequently is -- officer of several lodges.

So far I have dealt with the Tyler from what I may call the material point of view -- as the very practical officer of a very matter-of-fact institution.

But as a person stationed at the outside of the door of a Masonic Lodge he has another meaning which masons cannot afford to forget. A Lodge is regarded as a little center of light amid the darkness of the world; a little haven of good in the wilderness of evil; a little oasis of sweetness and love in the desert of life. The Tyler with his drawn sword is a perpetual reminder to us that nothing that is unworthy should be permitted within the sanctuary of the Lodge. Bro. J.T. Lawrence says there was a time when the Tyler s sword was "wavy" in shape, and he adds that it was thus made in allusion to the flaming brand placed at the east of the Garden of Eden, which turned every way to keep the way of the Tree of Life. When one remembers how rich our institution is in symbolism one may be inclined to accept Bro. Lawrence's statement as correct. It gives a dignity and an importance to the Tyler and adds a grandeur to the Lodge of which he is the keeper.

    The Tyler is armed with the sword for defense. He is to guard against the approach of cowans and eavesdroppers. He is to remain firm and do his duty. It is never his place to take the offensive. He waits the assault of the enemy and repels. In this connection it is maintained that the Tyler should never relinquish hold of the sword so that he may always symbolize the need for every Mason to be perpetually on his guard against the approach of unworthy thoughts and deeds.

    It follows from all this that the Tyler should be a commanding figure at the door of the Lodge.

Armed with his sword he should impress the postulant who seeks admission and when, later, that admission is gained, the candidate should learn just what the tyler's sword and office mean. They mark, as it were, the dividing line between the Lodge and the world. In a moral and spiritual sense they constitute the barrier between right and wrong. It is our common faith that the day will come when the light of truth shall gladden the whole earth, and our constant aim is towards the diffusion of that light. But so long as any territory remains under the power of darkness, so long as the Light of Masonry is not shed in the hearts of all men, so long will there be a barrier, so long will there be a dividing line, and so long will there be need for a Tyler with a drawn sword to guard the threshold of our faith.

The Mason's Apron

PREFACE

The Masonic Apron, as the badge common to all the brotherhood, has much to inspire reflection, and in the following pages I have brought together one or two thoughts upon the subject in the hope that they may be of use to members of the Craft.

4 Gowrie Street Dundee

THE MASON'S APRON

Probably the earliest moment at which a candidate for Freemasonry recognizes that he is really and truly a brother of the Craft is when the W.S.W. approaches him and in the name of the G.A.O.T.U., and by command of the R.W.M. invests him with the distinguishing badge of a Freemason. Whatever other information as to the Fraternity he may have gleaned from the outer world, he has certainly learned that Freemasons clothe themselves with aprons, and now when one of these articles of attire is girt about his waist he must realize that he is really within the pale of the brotherhood. The charge that follows the investiture whether it be the simple dignified little address that reads like a passage from Holy Writ or the more elaborate appeal which draws its color from the honors of Masonry and the jewels of the Eastern potentate cannot fail to impress him with the fact that the Fraternity looks upon the apron as a badge neither to be lightly conferred not to be worn with indifference.

As the apron is common to all the Degrees so it may be said with perfect truth that it is the most comprehensive symbol of our faith as well as the clearest evidence of our long descent. In a very material way it links us to those operative masons with whom we claim the closest kinship, and to whom we look as our immediate ancestors, but when it is invested with the attributes of innocence and purity it connects us in a community of thought and aspiration with the followers of every religion and the expounders of every moral system that has sought to elevate mankind.

The initiate is told that the badge is more ancient than the Golden Fleece or the Roman Eagle. Indeed, it is probably the oldest article of clothing in the world, and there is general agreement in the view that it was devised to preserve just that purity and innocence of which the Freemason regards is as an emblem. Out first parents in their earliest act of self-conscious pride wove fig leaves together to cover their nakedness, and this desire to veil the organs of creation is found as a natural instinct even among savage races. The grass skirt of the South Sea Islanders, the body cloths of the natives of India and Africa, and the conventional attire of civilized peoples may all be traced to this one primal instinct that it is good that a sense of innocence should be preserved.

It may have been just because of this moral significance that the apron was imported into religion and became one of the vestments of the priesthood. It is found as an article of the accepted dress of the priests of the Jewish faith, as well as of the officials of many other religions. The suggestion has been made that the apron is allied to the girdle of the prophets the girdle of Elijah in the Old Testament, and the girdle of John the Baptist in the

New. Both of these were of leather while is is also recorded that, on one occasion, Isaiah wore a girdle of hair-cloth, and that, on another occasion, Jeremiah donned one of linen. And it may have been that the priests borrowed the idea from the garments of the gods. Dr. Albert G. Mackey tells us in his Lexicon of Freemasonry that all the ancient statues of the heathen gods which have been unearthed in Greece, and Asia, and American are decorated with superb aprons.

If the Masonic apron is derived from early ecclesiastical clothing so also is its prevailing color. We read in the Book of Revelation that which is an emblem of purity and thus has it been esteemed in all ages. The Arch-Druid clothed himself in white ere he cut the sacred mistletoe; the priest of the Roman gods wore a vestment of white during the hour of sacrifice, and the priests of the Hebrew people wore ephods of white while engaged in the service of the sanctuary. These varying faiths met on the one common ground of making the white garment a symbol of the need that men should be pure in heart if they would enter into the presence of God.

Those Masonic students who like to trace all our Speculative system to the work of our Operative brethren say that as the Craftsman wore an apron to save his clothing from being soiled at work, so the Speculative brother dons it as a symbol of his desire to be kept unspotted from the world. But is has a longer lineage and a closer affinity with moral and spiritual purity than anything that can be drawn from the leather apron of the humble worker with mallet and chisel. Down through the ages a white garment has been the distinguishing feature of initiation. In the mysteries of Mithras in Persia the candidate was invested with a white apron, as he also was in certain Japanese initiations. The garment of initiation in Greece was of the same hue, because, says Cicero, white is a color most acceptable to the gods. As an emblem of holiness, the Essenians arrayed their postulant in a white robe which was bordered with a fringe of blue ribbon, and it may be a survival of this border that we have in the blue binding of some of our working aprons. If we pass from heathen to Christian practice we find the same color in evidence. It was customary in the primitive Christian Church for baptized converts to be impressively clothed with a white garment, and in that vision of the Grand Lodge above vouchsafed to the Apostle John at Patmos, we are told that there was a great multitude, which no man could number, out of every nation, and of all tribes and peoples and tongues, standing before the throne and before the Lamb, arrayed in white aprons.

I have said the apron is the most comprehensive symbol of our faith, and if, on the one hand it is derived from the garment which the Divine Creator bestowed upon fallen man in Eden, and on the other is an emblem of the robes of Paradise that have been washed and made white in the blood of the Lamb, then surely it is the fitting badge of the whole human race in their age-long march from darkness unto light!

And as that march of the whole creation is epitomized in the life of every individual it is fitting that the apron should be presented to the young Mason in the First Degree since his admission into the Craft in a state of helpless indigence is an emblematical representation of the entrance of all men on their mortal existence.

The Masonic Apron worn by the Initiate like everything else in our elaborate ceremonial, must conform to certain standards. It should be of pure white lambskin from fourteen to sixteen inches wide, and from twelve to fourteen inches deep with either a semi-circular or a triangular flap which falls to about four inches at its greatest depth. Often it is embellished with the name and number of the Lodge, but it should be without ornament of any kind. The yong Mason, accepting the plain undecorated apron as his chart, may trace upon it his upward career in the craft. When he reaches the Second Degree he may embellish it with two rosettes at the bottom, and when he becomes a Master Mason he may add a third rosette, line and edge it with silk of that color adopted by his Lodge, and further adorn it by adding tassels. The origin of tassels and rosettes has given rise to considerable discussion. It has been suggested that the tassels have been evolved from the two long ribbons by which early aprons were girt about the body. These ribbons passed round the waist and were tied under the flap, with the ends pendant in front. The ends were ornamented with a silver fringe, and had become so characteristic that, when the strap and buckle arrangement was devised, they were retained, being gathered up into the form of tassels and placed one on either side. No satisfactory explanation of the origin of rosettes has been furnished. One theory is that they represent the point within the circle with which all Freemasons are familiar, but it is not generally accepted. Other details, always in the way of more elaborate decoration, are added according to the taste of the wearer. Sometimes the rosette bears a five-pointed star in relief. Occasionally the flap is embellished with the compasses and square and the sacred symbol in the center. Now and again we find it ornamented with the Sun, the Moon, the Seven Stars, and the All-Seeing Eye. There does not appear to be any limit to the scheme of decoration which a brother may adopt so long as he confines himself to purely Masonic symbols. Office, of course, carried with it, its own ornaments. The apron of every office-bearer should display the particular jewel of his office; and in the case of a R.W.M. or P.M. the two rosettes at the bottom are replaced with levels of inverted Taus while the rosette on the flap gives way to the compasses and square enclosing the Sun and resting upon the segment of a circle, all which denote the rank of the brother.

But, no matter what the decoration or the rank it denotes every brother even the Grand Master upon whose honored shoulders rests the purple of the fraternity must bear in mind that no adornment can add anything to the moral grandeur of the symbol, and that the badge of a Mason is found not in fine gold nor in silken fabric, but in the pure and spotless surface of the lambskin which is the common mark as it should be the common object of veneration of every member of our ancient and honorable fraternity.

The thoughtful Freemason who lingers over the charge which is addressed to him at his investiture cannot fail to appreciate that the apron is an emblem of all that is highest and best in human life. Bro. W. Harry Rylands, in an article on The Masonic Apron, which he contributed to the Transactions of the Lodge Quatuor Coronati, says that he has found nothing which would lead him to believe that much of the symbolism of the Freemason s apron which is commonly received at the present time is of very early date. He inclines to the view that it may have come in when the newer symbolism was introduced as otherwise it would be difficult to account for so many aprons being made of silk, velvet, satin, cloth, canvas and even chamois- leather, which he suggests, with a touch of subtle humor, might be called the skin of the goat! But while lambskin and the moral teaching deduced therefrom may belong to modern Freemasonry, Dr. Oliver tells us that in ancient days the apron or girdle of whatever material composed was universally received as a symbol of Truth and all nations have ever regarded Truth as serenely throned upon a mountain high above the strife and turmoil of men and the warrings of races. Locke, the author of The Human Understanding , writing to Anthony Collins, says, to love truth for truth s sake is the principal part of human perfection in this world, and the seed- plot of all other virtues. We are told that the Apron is the badge of Innocence and the bond of Friendship. What is Innocence but the kindly smile on the face of Truth? And there cannot be any Friendship worthy of the name either between men or between nations that has not Truth as its one and only foundation. Friendship based upon anything else is but an Apple of Sodom fair to look upon and false when put to the test.

In addition to being the badge of Innocence and the bond of Friendship, the apron is an ever-present reminder of that purity of life and action which should at all times characterize a Freemason. The outer world, because it does not know us, regards us with rather dubious eyes. We are constantly wrapped about with an air of mystery and occasionally invested with an unworthy tradition; and if we were to seek to persuade the uninitiated that our mission was the uplifting of humanity they might smile in derision, and point a mocking finger. These things need not cause us to blush for the badge we don, nor deter us from our work in raising the Temple of character. Our legends tell us that the Master Architect was slain by men who could not appreciate the value of Truth and Honor, and the greatest Builder the world has ever seen was crucified at the behest of a mob who were blind to His great purpose. But the presence of three unworthy workmen at the Temple detracts in no way from the grandeur of the House which Solomon raised to Jehovah; just as the treachery of Judas, the denial of Peter, of the desertion of John in the Galilean drama dims not the glory of the sacrifice on Calvary. So if, in building the great temple of brotherhood, we meet with Masons who are not always true to their great ideals, that is no reflection upon the work to which we are called and no justification for the sneer and contempt with which many people, in their ignorance, regard Freemasonry. At the same time it is obvious that, if we would be true to the emblem which is our earliest tangible possession as Craftsmen, we must convince the world by exemplary conduct that merit is our title to the privileges we enjoy.

The Apron has inspired many, more or less indifferent poets to sing its praises, and, generally speaking , the effusions, like almost all Masonic verse, have hardly been worth the paper upon which they were printed. I came across some stanzas the other day entitled, The White Leather Apron, and while the poem as a whole was neither better nor worse than the generality of such things, I thought there was one quatrain that struck a rather inspiring note. After dwelling upon the fact that the badge was more ancient than the Golden Fleece and more powerful than the Field-Marshal s baton, the poet proceeded:--

Tis the shield of the orphan, the emblem of love,
Tis the charter of faith from the Grand Lodge above;
While the high and the low, in its witness arrayed,
Of one blood and one kin by its magic is made.

When first invested with it we are conjured to let its pure and spotless surface be to us an ever-present reminder of rectitude of life and purity of conduct; and a never failing argument for higher thoughts, nobler deeds, and greater achievements. What is all this but an appeal to the best that is in us to make this world a better place for ourselves and our fellow-men? The Freemason knows no party in politics nor does he confess any creed in religion, for, in theory as a member of a community, and in practice as an individual, he is willing to avail himself of whatever he can find in any party, and in every faith that tends to the uplifting of humanity. He takes the Temple of King Solomon as a symbol of that Temple of Ideals to the building of which he is called, but he does so only because he is a member of a brotherhood that has sought to give concrete form to its intangible design. Others are engaged in building the same Temple and are working with the same materials, for the stones are Truth, Honor, Friendship, and Purity, and the cement is Peace, Harmony, and Brotherly Love. It may be said, therefore, that all men are builders in a common cause, and yet in a very special sense the work is individual. In the erection of the Temple of Character it is not what other men do that counts. Other men may lay their courses well and truly but their work will reflect no credit upon us when the Master Architect comes to compare what we have done with what we were given to do. And it is just here that Freemasonry as an institution discharges its great function. By wealth of symbol and illustration it seeks to guide and direct its members in the paths of virtue and science, ever teaching them that the greatest happiness is found in doing good. Any good deed that I can do,: wrote someone who would not have dishonored Freemasonry, or any kindness that I can show, let me do it now: let me not defer it or neglect it, for I shall not pass this way again.

And that is the thought that should be in the mind of every brother who would prove himself worthy to wear the badge that is consecrated to goodness and virtue by centuries of usage. He has worn the Apron in vain who has not learned that our ancient Fraternity exists to shed the light of love upon this darksome world. In the Third Degree we are taught that a day will come when the apron will be put off never again to be worn on this side of eternity, and as there will be no building to be done by us when it is laid to rest beneath the silent clods of the valley,: it should be a constant reminder to us of the truth of the lines of Burns, our immortal bard and brother:--'

A few days may a few years must –
Repose us in the silent dust:
The voice of Nature loudly cries,
and many a message from the skies.
That something is us never dies;
That on this frail, uncertain state
Hang matters of eternal weight;
That future life in worlds unknown
Must take its hue from this alone;
Let us th' important Now employ,
And live as those who never die.

www.ingramcontent.com/pod-product-compliance
Lightning Source LLC
LaVergne TN
LVHW091322080426
835510LV00007B/605